Here are some horseba[…]
in temperament and pr[…]
reader a journey taken [...]
time. They move, often on four legs and mostly at a walk,
in terrain where loping and galloping is limited by both
gravity and treacherous footing. Some of them were
scribbled while perched on a log or a mat of juniper as
my horses grazed close by. Some were whittled down by
candle-light in remote patrol cabins, and later polished
under electric lights in distant cities. Starting in 1966,
it was my great privilege to be a backcountry warden
(ranger) in the Canadian Rockies and to spend most of
my time (from 1968 onward) on horseback, from June
to November, patrolling the mountain national parks.
To be candid, in the beginning it was the horses that
did the patrolling—I just went along for the ride. This
equine tutelage continued when my wife and I settled
in the ranching country of south-western Alberta at the
foot of the mountains. Today I am owned by two quarter
horses and they continue to furnish me with stories and
poems. I have selected poems from three earlier books,
Headwaters, *Nobody Danced With Miss Rodeo* and *Sky
Humour* to illustrate the various rites of passage of a life
lived close to the earth in the mountains and foothills
of British Columbia and Alberta, in the late decades of
the last century. The book concludes with newer material
that smacks of an even earlier time, since it is written in
the rhyming tradition that never went out of style on the
western ranges.

Other books by Sid Marty

Poetry
Headwaters (1973)
Nobody Danced With Miss Rodeo (1980)
Sky Humour (1999)

Non-fiction
Men for the Mountains (1978)
A Grand and Fabulous Notion (1984)
Leaning on the Wind (1995)
Switchbacks (1999)
The Black Grizzly of Whiskey Creek (2008)

The Rider
with
Good Hands

by Sid Marty

Frontenac House
Calgary, Alberta

Book and cover design: Epix Design
Cover Image: Author's collection
Author photo: Myrna Marty

Library and Archives Canada Cataloguing in Publication

Marty, Sid, 1944-
The rider with good hands / Sid Marty.

Poems.
ISBN 978-1-897181-45-4

I. Title.

PS8576.A795R54 2010   C811'.54   C2010-906701-0

We acknowledge the support of the Canada Council for the Arts for our
publishing program. We also acknowledge the support of The Alberta
Foundation for the Arts.

 Canada Council   Conseil des Arts
for the Arts   du Canada

Printed and bound in Canada
Published by Frontenac House Ltd.
1138 Frontenac Avenue S.W.
Calgary, Alberta, T2T 1B6, Canada
Tel: 403-245-2491 Fax: 403-245-2380
editor@frontenachouse.com   www.frontenachouse.com

Author contact: sid@sidmarty.com

To mountain horses;
long may they ramble through high-country meadows.

CONTENTS

Sky Humour – 1999

Buckshee – Songs And Verses

THE YEAR IS ANY YEAR

The loud boats are quiet in the arms of the shore
and the sun is spent, blown out by an evening wind
Then the nighthawk whirls and dips like an invisible top
plunged over the lake, and the fishermen are drunk
Too drunk to hear its whirling song

Wild horses gallop on the mountain trail
their manes crackle: the thunder walks up there

The year is any year, for engines have gone to sleep
Only the new moon rides these shadowy deeps

HEADWATERS – 1973

SPRING: INSIDE THE MAP
for Bob Haney

There is a trail into those ranges
its continuity more mapped than real
Constantly its aim is cut
by swollen creeks of runoff
Burdened by snow slides
it sags downhill

The forestry phone wire
is lost in a tangle
of trees and rocks
The voice fades
shorted through stone
filtered through roots
The twisted line breaks down

The warden there in spring
must cut his way out
then cut his way back in
Slashing away half thawed debris
Swimming his horses through lonely streams
Salvaging broken packs in the muck

Wet as a muskrat he rolls a smoke
thinking to strike the trail on the rock slide
Tightening a cinch, longing
for fire, his chilled gut
yearns for hot coffee
lashed with strong rum

Ten miles, twenty miles
Jacques Lake, Grizzly Shelter
Rocky Forks and mend corral
Reset horse shoes in the gumbo
Timber wolves howl up the valley
under Mount Balcarres

NIGHT CAMP BELOW MALIGNE PASS

Standing in the dark meadow
drinking coffee

The white bell mare gleams
in mountain shadow
Her bell clinking
a cold night in
The stars
vastly
shine in the metal
A tame bull moose
wades through willow

Campfire lights up the tent
Myrna throws a branch
upon the fire
On the trail
is the five-toed track
of a grizzly
"Our-Brother-Across-the-River"

Horses think of *Mustahyah*
and of getting by me
Though they're hobbled
they've learned
to jump
their front
feet
down the trail to home

DAWN: JINGLING PONIES*

Get up in faint cold light
Take some oats in a feed bag
Coffee will be ready when I return
Mist rising on the Maligne River

Half mile walk to toy horses
motionless in wet buck brush
silvered with frost
Feet get wet
to where they stand

White mare, the bell mare
shakes her head rings her bell
that Mac found twelve years gone
in distant mountains

In cold light and blue shadow
valley and mountain
their white blazes shine
While gentle mare takes the bit
untie the hobbles on one side
horses crowding round the feed bag
their warm breath on my neck
Ride back to camp, geldings following
their mare, ride bareback in the cold air
The mare's warm body
between my wet, chilled knees

*Alberta slang: To wrangle or gather up horses left to
graze overnight in the mountains.

LIGHTNING STORM

The forestry line is shorted out
has been for weeks
Picking up the ear piece
we hear
a thousand birds on a wire
miles apart
each in separate song
I don't know how this can be
while somewhere a lynx growls
from a lodge-pole pine
where a bird was singing
on an insulator

During the lightning storm
the bell rings slowly
on every strike
resistors smoke
The line to Jasper is out
The district warden's 30 miles up
the Little Cairn River
Hasn't been heard from
Can't be reached

Twelve spruce have fallen
on the lines near Beaver Cabin
In the morning, we'll be climbing
splicing wire, cutting deadfalls
with a chainsaw

Answering the switchboard's ring
I shout, "Do you need help?"
Far away a faint voice
fades in the sound of lightning
sound of wild cats in the timber

THE POCAHONTAS KID

Was the handle hung
on a young warden
in Pocahontas district
Jasper National Park

A palpable title
as the kid's voice
guivering on the radio was
"Worried about a flat tire"
they said, "or some knothead
five minutes late
from a mountain climb"

The kid's voice
giving off bad vibrations
amid the silence of the pine
and heat waves
Through smoke of forest fires
distant, and too terrible
to contemplate

His tenor rising a pitch
could bring tears of commiseration
"The sad sumahbitch"
they might say, frowning up
to distant hazy vistas
to fire lookouts
choking blind with smoke
impotent

Wishing they could
turn off the radio
"Jesus Christ"
they would swear softly
in the midst of shoeing a horse
Swatting huge
meat eating flies
amid horse farts
with a horse shoe nail
dangling from one lip
"Jethuth Chrithe"
they would say
almost fondly
The kid's voice echoing
in a distant truck

THROWING THE DIAMOND*
(for Bob Haney and Mac Elder)

Throwing the diamond
for the first time
though only on a dummy horse
built of a rusty barrel
held up by hay wire
to four pines

A pack saddle, pack baskets
and for a top pack
the box from the Moose's salt lick
while he stands back there
dumbfounded, but austere
the Great Canadian Fable, unsung

> Yesterday, I felt
> about as useful
> as teats on a stallion
> while Bob packed
> three horses single-handed
> (not bad for the space age)
> jumped in the saddle
> and cocking his hat
> rode away for the Rocky River

But today I've learned
the shaman knot
that makes a horse jump logs
and cliff-bands
Following anywhere
once he's packed
Knowing he needs
your magic hands
to conjure that burden
off his back
Cause he'll buck and sunfish
but the load stays on
with a well tied diamond

"Three horses" said Mac
"is nothing. Why I've packed
twenty head and more alone

"They'd follow me anywhere once tied
up and down mountainsides
on the geological survey
through muskeg up to their arseholes

"And there's seven kinds of a diamond
I've shown you the easiest only ...
But this here haywire horse you've tamed
must be
'bout the meanest sonofabuck
I ever did see"

*Diamond Hitch: A famous rope hitch used in horse
packing.

PACKING DYNAMITE

"The thing to remember"
he said
Bull Durham bag suspended
archly from one pinky
"is to keep your dynamite
and your blasting caps
in two separate places"

Caps were in my saddlebags
dynamite packed on the mare
And back and forth my horses
battled for the lead
banging pack-box and saddle
roughly together
eight miles up the river
to the camp above Twin Falls

My sun tan flaked off
and I was a white and shining angel
ready to take wing
All in white pieces
of a horse shit bomb

SIWASHING*
(for Al Purdy)

This is what I would do
if the down timber
stretched to the sky
Siwashing, my mind
on a jumping horse
toward a sunset
not only breaking down
but torn away
Riding for the ragged curtain

Is what I do
born fifty years too late
Will not get used to
dying on a cushioned seat
rolling down my grey tomorrows

So I ride these mountains
through the widowmakers
carrying away old snags
that catch on my leather

Had I fringes
I would wear them
all torn up by timber
to flash in the shintangle

Call it 'siwashing'
What we do out here
when we need to go through places
that do not seem desirable

Eye weeping
hat torn
one spur broken
gun butt catching on limbs
half unsaddled
the pony mad, and
flies would eat your socks

And it feels like a saga
so it is
To live your own story
is no lie

It feels strong
it burns the loins
the sun's whip-like motion
through the spruce

Here
is a cliff edge
and
there
is a muskeg hole
There
is the track of a bear

Twist, dodge
turn archaic
half forgotten skills
to service

When the old men all are gone
you must teach it to yourself
And siwashing
that all consuming art
was good enough
for me

* Slang expression, Alberta mountains: Traveling on
horseback through rough terrain without established
trails.

SHAWN

You're an old horse
angrily willing yourself to die

From four in the morning till midnight
we packed the trail crew's food and tents
down from Twin Falls in the rain
It had to be suicide for me
but for your last fibres of restraint
on the black, two-foot wide trail
switch-backing down the side-hills,
the two mares, tied nose to tail
biting your flanks
to push us to death, or home

You held them when a halter broke
while I slid blindly among their legs
searching, knife in hand
Then carried me on, down the dark mountain's head

The river was a snake hissing at your heart
Your iron shoes clattered on stone
in the sparkling darkness
But you're tired of saving my skin

They were glad to see us
the trail crew, huddled under soggy spruce
by the midnight creek

But at their greeting you reared
pulled back
the halter bruising, the bit
twisting, cutting your mouth

Your eyes roll wild from the lantern's flame
and the crew grieves for the old man
tearing from light with bloody lips

Furiously retreating into night

TOO HOT TO SLEEP

He was sleeping when bear
came down from the mountain
(by the water trap)
after cleaning the screen
of branches and gravel

He fell asleep, a hot June morning
above Wapta Lake, the Kicking Horse Pass
When *Muskwa* came down without a sound
and snuffed at his jeans

Who's this asleep on my mountain

"It's my friend Birnie asleep," I said
(in my head)
"I didn't hear you coming bear
I was dozing, I looked up
and there you were."

You never know said Bear
just where the wind will lead me
when I'll be around
or what beat I'm hunting on

And sniffed at Birnie's collar
at his ear, which he licked tentatively
causing Birnie to moan softly

Nothing doing here he said, nothing doing

"We were just going bear," I said quietly
edging backwards

Don't move too quickly will you, said Bear
when you move, or better still
don't move at all

Are you here often, are you coming again?
he asked, flipping over a stone
licking delicately the underside
"No," I said. Good he said, that's good

I just came down from the pass
the wind blowing up my nose
to see who was sleeping on my mountain
he said, and sniffed at Birnie's armpit
Whoosh—Whoosh he snorted

Then turned away, clattered down the creek
popping his teeth, his hackles up
Went out of sight there
on the shoulder of Mount Hector

As Birnie woke up rubbing his eyes
"Too hot to sleep," he said.

"Yeah"
  I
 said

LOW PASS

A man once came this way
and I think I know him
following his blazes
years behind him

A Whiteman
No Indian would need
to mark these trees
or look in the water
to recall his own face

For in these meadows
he was lonely
It is remembered in silences
that bluebells
hurt him,
and the fields
of blue-eyed Mary
black-eyed Susan

A wind
a woman's touch
on his shoulder

Sometimes I lose track
fooled where a bear
blazed a tree
sharpening up
Stop,
Make a circle
find the right way

Look back, remember
how it looks
Then, to his next blaze

Moving up, ghost guided
Moving on

AUGUST: THE MOON OF RIPE BERRIES

Late August and the going better
the trail mud pounded flat by horse and deer
Half asleep in the steep ascent
the thud of hooves rouses me
A brown bear, full of loganberries
rattles the steaming thickets in his course

Duchesnay Lake trail
free of the water now
Pack horse nipping at my wheezing pony

They stiffen, ears up
as a rutting moose charges
knee high through the blue shallows
behind us, a horny juvenile
kicking up rainbows
cooling in Duchesnay water

Rank moosewa in their nostrils
spooks the horses. I speak softly
We dance through a tangle of deadfalls
I push in my spurs
The gelding rolls his eye backward
and shows his sage old teeth

He remembers the elbow
in his ribs yesterday
when he stepped on my foot
He still has much to teach me
and I've a lump for each lesson

High water has choked the trail with snags
My last chore in the summer ending
bucking the snags by Duchesnay water

The chainsaw breathes out a blue smoke
Cool air fills with the roar of the motor
but horses sleep on their feet regardless
The bear comes to see them
they are not impressed
Runs off, coughing, when the saw stops

At the end of the meadow
the wind has abandoned the lake
and muscles through the timber
Spruce needles fall from the boughs
where my mare rubs her cheek
on the rough, sticky bark
showering the upturned petals
of orange paintbrush

The bear returns from his solitary harvest
prowling across my tracks
smelling the ripeness
of big spruce, toppled and broken
three feet thick, promise of beetles
or fat spruce budworms

In the quiet now
is the continuous pattering
of ripe fruit falling
on thick duff
of the forest floor

A SEARCH

Turns out the man with epilepsy
did not die alone up Meadow Creek
but having missed the trail completely
he crawled over a mountain range
and came down on the highway
near Dominion Prairie

And turns out the man I tracked
down Meadow Creek in the rain
Horse attempting to present me
with close ups of muddy terra
Was just some phantom fisherman
or wild spook wandering
crazed through the greenery

  But I did meet a wrangler
  at nightfall
  who'd ridden in from Jasper
  And we exchanged opinions
  on lost horses and fools
  near Maccarib pass
  and the grave of Warden Goodair
  killed by a grizzly in 1929

While the moon shone
through a mist of fine snow falling
on the antlers of a deer by the water
on two lovers alone by a fire
and on me, riding five miles
over wet shining stones to hear
horse bells shivering
over the meadows

COYOTE AGAIN

Coyote keeps his real name secret
so no one gets that handle to beat him with

He's seen *Mustahyah* rubbed out
and offered a bowl of his own liver
in tribute from his killers

Mustahyah, skinned out
looking like a heavy muscled man
A naked man, with talons

Coyote's flesh is ranker than a carcajou's
His hide is full of fleas
Even a starving Methodist missionary
spurned the flesh of the yellow dog

Coyote pisses on the strychnine baits
to warn off other creatures
He steals the bait from the leghold traps
and turns them over
He wrecks the snares set for *Sehkos*
the weasel, and sometimes gets caught
Gets his head clubbed in

Returning in other pelts, he walks
over the graves of pious men
sniffing out secret vices

Goes on living, closer to the town
each year, until he winds up
feeding in the alleys of night
a jump away from the bush or prairie

Full of pride, he makes up melodies
to multiply his saga, a skilled ventriloquist
moving in from all directions at once

He sings, breeds gleefully
with any cur he finds
and prospers accordingly

He eats whatever he runs down
He eats the afterbirth of the deer
He eats shit when times are hard
or tells fortunes from it with his nose

He eats the bones of *Mustahyah*
thrown on the dung heap behind the corral

RIDING OUT OF ROCKY FORKS COUNTRY

Ten days on the boundary
the black mare's knees swell up
erupt in yellow pus
so it's decided to bring her out
through Cairn Pass
down the river, the Medicine Tent

From the outpost, Grizzly Shelter
a trail runs through willow, through alder
by the river, and rich soapberries
good bear food grows there

Rode singing in a light rain

There was bear scat, full of red berries
track of the little stocky brown
three or four years old, wears
a cinnamon mantle
on his thickset shoulders

Ranging the valleys, he's wild
disdaining the highway
He combs the side-hills
strong as a young spruce, fat
with pounds of wintering lard

His spoor is fresh
The tracks ooze water
as he prowls ahead of me
and once he barks beside me
somewhere in a dogwood thicket
The horses' ears swivel slowly
trained on him like radar cones

Keep moving, Little Brother
I say, to let him know who's coming
It is he
I smell his rank musk
and he's heard my voice
before

Don't mess with us
I warn him
This black mare kicks like thunder
poor little bear
and with my saddle axe
I'd split your skull
should you choose to close
this distance, clearly
we have you outnumbered
I tell him, and I know

There is no fear to smell on me
Ten days horse sweat and stiff jeans
that stand up by themselves

So I keep on singing though
Little Brother offers no trouble
His presence makes me cunning
cold with a cold rain
and quick moving

I will sing my song for him
and this weather
Brother, we will travel together
deadheading down, unseen
to each other
as you lead me to the road

Brother, we will sound each other
when the wind shifts

We shall be certain
of one another
Brother bear

PUSHING THE BOUNDARY

On the boundary
we stare down
the crossfire world
bending from the foothills
and prairie
Out where they hunt
with impunity
Taking their guns
from jeweled scabbards
sighting into the sky

In here we declare
only the animals
may kill each other
Sometimes
may even kill us

But it's hard to draw
the boundary
imaginary line
that cuts the watersheds
You have to know the ground
climb the crumbling mountain walls
to know which way the rivers run
Headwaters, where the world begins

Magic bullets
sing straight
through any flesh
weighted with ink to paper

The Big Horn rams
dragging their broken
hindquarters
over the finish line
do not believe it
seeing my revolver

Of square miles
I've a thousand to cover
Like a wolf on the prowl
I leave tracks in the passes
so the killers will know
there's a killer riding the boundary

My markers at various summits
I often find riddled with bullets
but I smile
The shots come from outside

And dressed all in green
I float among the trees
Staring out on the plains
of September
to hear the distant roll of guns
draw near

TOBY

Got a picture of you
with my arm around your neck
and you dejected
It being a heavy arm
and a heavy man
to lug around the mountain sides
of Tonquin Valley

Guess I worked you pretty hard
that last month, when the snow
was getting deep
Scared you a few times, too
crossing rock slides
veined with ice

Looking for the angry grizzly sow
Who'd treed two hikers in the Tonquin
and happy not to find her, too
we were

I was glad to be on a horse
One with a good nose, and strong legs
like yours
and a bear could hear or smell you
farting miles away

In a letter they tell me
now you are dead
with seventeen horses
all lost
The fever killed you

And I recall your trembling legs
and that your shoes needed pulling
but the work that year was over

And I was anxious
to get out of the cold
So I stripped my tack
and bribed you with oats
Goodbye, in the muddy corral

Now I write these tear jerker lines
for an animal, a beast of burden
I worked with
and depended on
who was my friend
from depending
on me

HAY MEADOW CREEK

Many horses die in winter range
on Hay Meadow Creek
under the shadow of Devil's Head mountain
Ranges of the eastern wall
mark their bones, where clear water
flows through the white frames

Fishing for brook trout
we heard the wetlands beat
to the hooves of half-wild horses
Brewster's wrangler in buckskin
chased ponies weary of dudes
desiring only to join the wildies
take their chances with weather, run free

Told us the grass was scarce
the snow deep
Old horses get weak going for water
get down, can't move
and wearily drown

Fishing for trout among clean bones
where a beaver swam out
Muskrats lived in his round house
A day of sunshine, hail, then rain

At night we baked fish
The coyotes, hearing the dog bark
howled, surrounding our camp
Out there they look in
seeing fire's red star
Their voices suspended
ride the flat, cold air
driving the dog mad
out of the firelight
We caught him in the timber
shut him in the truck

First star over the Devil's Head
The coyotes, running in circles
bark for joy
since clear nights promise a late snow

Out on the old horse graveyard
the last trout jumps
and the ripple
fades into blackness
goes out

*NOBODY DANCED WITH
MISS RODEO – 1981*

WHEN I JOINED THE OUTFIT

When I joined the outfit
they issued me
a 30-30 lever action rifle
20 rusty bullets, binoculars
a saddle and a bridle

With two old
but fool-killing horses

And a log house
in which I found
a package of noodle soup
three Hudson's Bay blankets
and no maps
to tell me where to begin

The house was where
the roads
stopped

When I joined the outfit
they gave me
Four-hundred square miles of
rivers, lakes
glaciers, mountains

The key to all the gates
They said lock them all
behind you,
I had
Time
to travel in,
Peace
of mind

THERE WAS A LADY MET A BEAR
(in Jasper National Park)

There was a lady met a bear
The lady, wearing cold cream
Was lying naked in a tent
Beside a mountain stream

This lady had a sunburn, and
I should have said before
How really terrified she was
When the bear came through her door

So quietly, on padded feet
With expression somewhat bored

There must be fats in cold cream
and oils that black bears love
– Someone should do a study
(They probably already have)

Perhaps it's high in protein too
– I really do not know
But the black bear licked this lady
in her tent, so cool and shady
The black bear licked the lady
From her head down to her toes

The lady didn't scream, oh no
But, terrified, lay still
Trembling 'neath the black bear's tongue
Which seemed insatiable

And when the black bear ambled off
She dressed, got in her car
And hurried to the nearby town
To buy another jar

THE SPUR

An overbearing wind
clawed and roared through the spruce

And a blue butterfly
fertilizing flowers
was blown off course
to cling on my hat

The year was 1975
but I was still riding a horse
– part time

The horse was a victim of its desires
would not comply with my gentle hands

Three times a jet plane flew over
Three times the wild horse threw me
into the cinquefoil shrubs

This horse and I were thousands of feet
high up a mountain valley
where the stones among the flowers
are the tips of slowly rising mountains

Where the stones are sharp among the flowers

Where Incongruity's palpable
plateaus announce themselves
draw blood

Now I had a pistol in my saddlebags
(tools of the trade)
but I had left the bullets at home

So in my humility, I took off my hat
tried to caress those translucent wings
ever so gently with one, bleeding finger
But reality had settled there
like the beginnings of fever

Like the ripples of a sonic boom

The horse shied – again
And I knew that my humility
was arrogance.No match
for beauty's diaphanous disguise

And I spread my scarecrow wings
I crowed my fury to the wind

Then the horse went up in the air – again
And came down, up and down

But I taught him, with the spurs
what I had learned
among the flowers
I sat him till he stopped

Till he was trembling with fear
And I loved him, for his hatred
was pure, weightless and winged

So sure was I of him
that I thought I'd fly him home

That was several years ago
and maybe long before

My butterfly
had flown

THERE JUST AIN'T NO RESPECT

There's a vacuum cleaner
in the middle of the hall,
I whispered icily to her dark form
breathing in the warm bed

Is there? She murmured huskily
hiding her hostility
beneath a fake allure
Knowing full well there was

She'd left it there
An act of mutiny
against the pernickety laws
of good housekeeping

Daring me to notice

Well, my leg's in a cast at the time
I'd broken it at work
on avalanche control
(We dropped dynamite in snowdrifts
the government paid us for this)
I tried to chop down a tree
with one ski, while my foot
was still attached
outrunning an amorous snow-slide

So all day I crutch
nimbly over the Electrolux
like a three legged pole-vaulter
without complaint
until I gleefully forget the thing is there

All night I lie with ankle throbbing
thinking how they murdered Garcia Lorca
Thinking that Marty is also Martyr
(just add an "r")
At four a.m. I get up to stretch
Damn thing is killing me

Check the kid's blankets she says
sleepily

Well, it's pitch black in the old rhythm ranch
and my mind's full of wondrous poetry
When I hit that vacuum cleaner
waiting in the dark for me   .
That steel torpedo
wired for pain
That metal crocodilc
with its flailing nylon tail

And the song I sang
was the song of the iron piano

The Spanish Civil War whizzed
right out of my mind
As stars shoot through
a dark red cloud

There just ain't no respect
for poets, in this world
or the next

I cut my toe...
I'm tracking blood on the cold floor
But I don't cry out, being
a hardened husband, just
cover the babies
my teeth clenched
and limp back to bed

To hiss at her who huddles by the wall
There's a vacuum cleaner
in the middle of the hall

To which she answers, triumphantly
I know. Whew! Your feet are cold

I lie there, feeling like dead Lorca
executed by powers he didn't recognize
Or in my case the merely homicidal mate

Remembering the folly
of dancing on my cast
while drunk, to demonstrate
the Cripple's Two-step

Breaking the thing in mid-caper
(Somehow it got soaked with rum)
So a nurse, with a saw reciprocal
cut it off, with a smile elliptical
that promised more pain to come

I'm wide awake, for sure
That flower of womanhood
she lies in the dark, asleep
I can hear her gently breathe

The scent of her is all
rose petals and morphine dreams

I move that way
Arms and legs surround me
warmth dissolves the pain
slowly
    Into
            sleep, and

Here comes the ghost of a poet
chasing me with a vacuum cleaner
spouting an avalanche of poems

Hovering and hoovering, it must be
Lorca!
Damn it all, Lorca,
Stop laughing at these humble metaphors...

FOR MY SONS

Two boys in my lap,
and I've become a horse
a swing, a raft on a creek,
the strong limb of a tree
poised over a hay stack

Sitting at my poems
trying to engage the imagination
As they crawled up my chair
and made me
a creature of theirs

THE FORDING

A woman and a boy ride down into Bryant Creek
They water their horses at the ford
under the glacier brow of Mount Eon

My wife and my son, strangers in weathered hats
sit their horses and talk in the middle of the stream
of the things that beautiful women and small boys
talk of, there where the wind blows the first buds
of the cinquefoil, and trout skip forward
from the billowing mud under a horse's foot
to glitter in the clear again

I would be like those quick gleams
to be always shining for their eyes and hearts
A selfish man. But I can't help longing
to be held with them in their perfect moment
needed to frame this day, as they frame mine

How their yellow slickers trail along the wind!
I watch and build an answering fire
here at the clearing's edge.

They turn toward the smoke and canter
my living lights, the fire of my days
Shining motes are we, below the massed green timber

With a whoop, with a shout
they are riding toward me now
Smashing the dewy alder shrubs to rainbows
over a plain of trembling orange flowers
Making me cry aloud at their fatal beauty
Go running forward to meet them, and surrender

WHEN I LEFT

Twelve years rolled by
Not all of it was memorable
When I left the outfit, they
didn't ask me why
I told them anyway

They gave me
a refund on my pension
eight months late, and
without interest
My old and bloodstained
climbing boots for a souvenir
They kept the rifle
the horses the cabin
and they changed the locks
(I think the packrats ate my blankets)

I left because they murdered
the peace that I had found

And handed me a photograph
of a mountain

SKY HUMOUR – 1999

THE RIDER WITH GOOD HANDS
(In memorium, David Billington)

In the falling snow
in the field below the garden
A man and a horse are arguing
about barrels, empty barrels in the yellow grass

The rider with good hands
tall in his sheepskin coat
his long black hair dusted with snow
Knows that cavalcades
of horsemen who have ridden here before
are riding here again, through him

His hands upon the reins can check
rebellion in a stubborn mouth
and not give pain. He knows
how the best horses run

How to collect imaginary terrors
trembling between his knees
and turn them into dance

He is a student of arts, roughhewn
but true, and this horse (unruly
as the first draft of a story
or a song) must make
one perfect figure eight

Before the patient rider lets it go
back naked to the windy field, to run
its wild gymkhanas with the sun

A perfect figure, done cleanly

And though at last it was stamped down
Though it was covered in a moment by the snow

I see the rider, still,
flowing on four dancing feet
over the sheer dazzle
of an endless, white page

His hands talking tough
talking gentle through the lines
His heavy body lifted
by the beauty of his knowledge
into grace

THE DAM

Three years before the dam
they took our names from the district map
We're in the way; they want us to un-be

They took my bottom land
in a bumper year for hay
Our water goes to Lethbridge
sixty miles away

I went into the town
and saw their faces slick with greed
They yap of progress as they steal
Two years of boom and to hell
with generations of a rancher's trade

I thought of violence, and the law
(It's never been our way)
I took my title out
and threw it to the fields

I know we stole this land before
Those tipi rings
will soon be under water
with the bare foundations of our kin

Before they drowned our memory
they stripped the soil away
I felt it coming off me
like a second skin

I'm raw and giddy
Moving in such pain
I'm like a tumbleweed
Roots torn up
and waiting for the wind

AT THE BREAKING OF DROUGHT

Steam rises from the mud
The wind has banked two months of heat
into this cracked clay

After a late night rain
even the shadow of a crow
smells fresh

A white bull beside the road
rises like a monument
So clean, so sharply is it drawn in air
when the dust is wetted down

A cow in the fir tree's shade
turns its head today
as if it feels alert

As if it's interested
in my transit through its brain

As if there were a thought

AT THE FALLS
(a lyric from the album Let the River Run)

Down by the falls
she bent to swim
Where the limestone dipped
to lead her in

Raspberries spill
down on the bank
and everything that lives
gives thanks

Down by the river, as we stripped
I held a handful to her lips

I painted a turtle on her thigh
"You'll be a living pictograph"
Her laughter rolled from cliff to cliff

Because my mouth was drought
so dry, that no water satisfied

She crushed the berries on my tongue
and with her kiss, I drank them in

Then we rolled in the water
down to the sand
To the painted gravel
where the rainbows spawn

The red juice melted in the flood
She held me then in another mood

Raspberry mouth in the river's lift
Rosebuds float at her tawny breasts

And the blue river in her eyes
As the water laughed and cried
Our ponies listening
when a voice, in the earth, began to sing

LUNAR ECLIPSE

Now the moon in her brief purdah
takes the veil of grey mist

Then the coyotes stop singing
though the mountain wind thunders
its endless train

Down by the gate
some shapeless beast is waiting
My old dog presses against my knee

The moon has broken her promise to be free
of the traps set by the sun
What was known has been suspended
What can be known, not yet invented

The last beam fades down to a pin prick
The beast remains against the starlight
Is it the mare who knows my touch
or a moose, browsing on constellations?

The moon's in purdah; the world is new
and strange

Reach out your hand, to touch
the enchanted monster

Startled, it shies on the dark gravel
striking sparks with its iron shoes
It had forgotten you, your hammer
and your noose

But when the naked moon returns
She rides the white mare, trembling, home

BALLAD OF THE ONION
(to an editor)

At lunch we ordered salad
Serene, and spare of build
she gazed upon the legumes
while her water glass was filled

But she edited the
"un-yens!"
like unwanted exclamations
from the paragraphs of lettuce
and the carrot's ex-
plications

She asked to see some
"poe-hems"
I read for her that night
The verses stripped me naked
I was blinded by her light

But she left the crowded room
with a speed that seemed
rehearsed
It must have been the
onions
stinking up the verse

A letter came today,
her writing is so
neat
Reminds me of the way
she nibbles vegetables, sans meat

She sent me back the
Poe-hems
"Try again some day
We only use postmodern
and rhyming is passé "

I still can smell the perfume
of this literary seer
Who condescends to smile
when she prefers to sneer

Her pearly teeth, her crimson nails
once pierced me to the core
But many a beast that chews a leaf
has the heart of a carnivore

STEVE

Steve is out in the raw wind
sawing boards from a pallet
salvaging hardwood to smoke some meat
wasting nothing

He built this ranch from a miner's wages
Hard work purchased more hard work

Good natured, he forgives my trade
my life of words not real to him
for whom work means everything

He hays our little field, lends me his tractor
helps us skin and split an elk each fall
Very little Steve and Rosy wouldn't do
to help a neighbour. They're the kind
that feed this nation

He says there's work at Forestry
"Why doncha go cut them beetle-bug trees?"

I talk of deadlines, writing scripts
it makes him blush

I know he's thinking as I leave
"The poor bugger's got nothing to do"
In his torn parka with the ragged sleeves
does he pity me, my neighbour Steve?

HUNTING ELK

I don't hunt for sport
that's why I hunt alone
I'd take the oldest one
if he wants to learn

That one has feelings, though
He can draw things, so quick!
But let a creature die
and he'll mourn it in his sleep

Tonight the elk are out
those brown dots on the ridge
west, above the house

At dawn they will drift north
into the thickest firs
I've tracked them there before

The snow is knee high there
and drifted to the waist

I'll have to be gone by six
It's best I go alone
up to the valley's head

I'll have to be waiting there
where the elk lie down

A PRAYER IN LIEU OF WINDCHIMES

There's a cap of cloud on the Livingstone
Pushed by a waterfall of air
cloud pours over that brim of rock
The wind sleds down to the valley below
to whoop-up gravel on the Burmis road
which rattles, like hail, on a passing truck

Chinook is quarrelling with my roof
and on the path
it polishes the snow to ice
so down I crash
I call it a homicide underfoot
but I'm still alive, so I have no proof

The school-bus gets a hearty gust
that blows it over into the ditch
The kids escape, though one or two
are hunted down by the wild Chinook
rolled arse over teakettle under a fence
yet never catch their hide on a barb
So the wind's not blowing all that hard

The cottonwood that fell in our yard
had stood these shocks a hundred years
Oh what a terrible blow to the house
that would have been; but it missed us, clean
I cannot call Chinook a fiend
though like a banshee I hear it keen

I wondered why my neighbour installed
that picture window, facing west
He knows the giant that rules this scene
hates to be mirrored while venting its spleen

Today it shattered under a blast
No one was hit by the flying glass
though shards were speared in the living-room wall
The roof only shifted ten inches back
off its plate; I'd say it stood the attack
of a wind that can hurl a train from its track

If the wild Chinook ever really blew
it would peel the earth up like a rug
Send houses, ranches fields and farms
to roll right over Saskatchewan
Get down to bedrock, and carve some flutes
to celebrate and sing its songs

And so it's a charm, or a prayer to say
in lieu of the windchimes, which blew away
I'm glad the wind's not blowing today

Amen, to the sleepy little hurricane
gnawing on the spine of the Livingstone Range
Hooping up a windsock from a logging chain
Circling, circling, rounding up strays

But I'm glad the wind's not blowing today

MR. DITTY WAH DITTY
(For Ry Cooder and lonely
writers in res, Banff Centre)

They put this washing machine in here
to test my patience
And when it started bopping and moaning
crazily unbalanced once too often

I mounted up and rode the spin cycle
all around that log kitchen
pounding its sides and hollering

I'M OUTTA THE CHUTE, LET 'ER BUCK

My dear, I was thinking of you
while beating a cowboy jazz riff
to the song of the paddle that goes

Duh diddlydum, duh diddlydum, duhdiddly wah doo

On a long cord
The coloured lights were flashing
and
just past the living room door
I went flying, bucked into the
 IKEA jungle
of pine sticks and burlap

But in a great autogasm
of frolicking blue jeans
and spilled underwear

The big, high-yellow beauty
pulled the plug and took the stairs
rolling like homemade thunder
down the mountain to Banff Avenue

To interface more meaningfully
with *deus ex machina*

Left me lyin' here cryin'
Come back and tumble me dry

Diddlydum, duhdiddly dum
Ditty wah ditty
(Repeat if necessary)

BARBED WIRE

1.

My gloves are more ethereal than real
reduced to air and ragged leather
by wire, writhing on its hooked scales
between the posts, pulling the hills together

I stretched it with a come-along, too taut
I heard its warning hiss
It broke, and came back to my arms
with its rasping kiss

My life becomes so simple now
It makes me shiver
My veins coil and slip
like wires on posts
The posts in the distance seem like slivers

The trees are mine now, brides
leaning from green beds
never brought to labour. No more
they'll mosey with my horses
into alien fields of night
(Bad fences make bad neighbours)

2.

I love to hear the tractor moan
when the power-take-off cuts in
To rein its lunging in with one hand
while sucking blood from a wire cut
This is the way I make my eucharist

A tractor is a horse that eats diesel fuel
instead of oats. The kind that might
kick you into eternity
while driving posts

Just for a moment there, feeling religious
I forgot the mountain slowly rising
underneath this sod. Six feet of pine
cut last fall, shattered under the pounder
whispered past my ear, and tumbled
through the buttercups. The petals burst
and fell in silent notes of brilliant laughter

The season winds out endless snares
we are as much closed out as in
Meanwhile the mare is fenced out of our garden
No more rolling through the broccoli for her

A red hose leaks hydraulic blood
The front-end-loader bows and sinks
its jaws into the grass

There's a bead of dew along the silver wires
Each tiny knife is poised to teach the flesh
the one lesson tired nerves will not let pass

BUCKSHEE
Songs and Verses

LITTLE SAILOR

The moon is but a ghostly galleon
Weakly shining through canyons of cloud
Tonight the stories flowed like whiskey
And I'm a long way from town

Mountains lean through sprinkled stars
to hear me think aloud
About love and loss and what it cost
to be a stranger in the crowd

Roll on Little Sailor
Mountain pony, lead the way
You've saved my hide so many times
That I never can repay
Sail us home today

Just a stocky little bay horse
Loved to kick his heels and go
"Ain't much to look at," said the barn boss
"But he's got a heart like a stove"

When they handed me the halter
Been mistreated by a greenhorn, I could see
And I had to eat some dirt
Before he put his trust in me

Roll on, Little Sailor
Mountain pony, lead the way
You've saved my hide so many times
That I never can repay
Sail us home today

On a sandbar as the night fell
Tracks of that big old silvertip
But since you've grazed
Next to him before
You and I don't give a rip

All too well you know my habits
When I get out on a spree
You've grazed all night around my feet
While I slept beneath a tree

The trail is but a phantom's ribbon
That I can barely see
But if I can smell that grizzly bear
He can sure as hell smell me

Roll on, Little Sailor
Mountain Pony, lead the way
You've saved my hide so many times
That I never can repay
And when we get to Barrier
You'll get your fill, of oats and hay
Sail us home, today

AN OUNCE OF PREVENTION

Farewell Dormer Mountain
And the old Short Cut Trail
Farewell to the white goats
Out on the black shale

And you mountain ponies
Traversing the cliffs
Where there's nothing to catch us
But pillows of mist

Just an ounce of prevention
Used to keep him in line
Patrolling the precincts
Of Wild Mountain Thyme

Now the poachers are riding
The backcountry trails
But Jim's in the Legion
Riding on the brass rail

Farewell Totem Creek
And those carvings he made
Of fierce hearted warriors
And big busted maids
From the shadowy old-growth
Their faces would stare
Ambushing the pilgrims
And the grizzly bears

Just a bit of discretion
And he would have been fine
If he'd kept his obsessions
In the back of his mind

But he rode into town
And he danced the wolf dance
Bit a lovely ski bunny
On her lovely ski pants

To the old mountain outfit
I bid you adieu
Couldn't stay out of trouble
Though I've been trying to

Since the Second World War
And that bloodbath in France
Hiding out in these mountains
Was my only chance

With so many trying
To be somebody else
My only desire
Was to just be myself

You can stick your brass badge
Where the sun doesn't shine
I'll go back to the ranches
And ride the grub line

Farewell Dormer Mountain
And the old Short-Cut Trail
Farewell to the white goats
Out on the black shale

And you mountain ponies
Traversing the cliffs
Where there's nothing to catch us
But pillows of mist

OTHER PEOPLE'S CATTLE

I met an old man on the streets of town
He didn't look to me like he belonged
Bought him a drink that winter night
He told me something of his life

He said my money's getting lonely, from lack of company
And my old truck is tired of defying gravity
The kids all call me "Patches," as 'round this town I go
I blame that on my mother, for teaching me to sew
And I'm all stove up from fifty years
Of days spent in the saddle
I spent the best years of my life
Raising other people's cattle

I went down to the wishing well and threw a penny in
A face I didn't recognize, looked up at me and grinned
But I get dressed up for Leo's bar, I take a weekend chance
I'm too old for the ladies – but I'm not too old to dance
Though I'm all stove up from fifty years
Of days spent in the saddle
But some of them were good days, too
Raising other people's cattle

It must be thirty years ago
Ginny's pony hit that badger hole
I cursed myself, I cursed my god
But Ginny whispered – "It's not your fault"
Our son lives in the city now
And so I've carried on it seems
It's not as lonely as you think
She comes to hold me in my dreams

I'd hate to calculate the miles of barbed wire
I've strung. Beloved stock dogs I've outlived
The ponies I've worn down
And they laugh to see what the sun can do
To this weathered old red neck
Or how the rope that took my thumb
Has left my hands a wreck

But I wouldn't trade my memories
You know the townie makes me shiver
He drinks his whole life from a glass
Well, I drank from the river

My riding roping days are done
(I don't know why I keep that saddle)
We helped to feed this country, boys
Raising other people's cattle